HELLO GOD

Can You Hear Me?

Vickie Fisher

Author and Photographer

Copyright © 2022 by Vickie Fisher

Hello God, Can You Hear Me?
by Vickie Fisher

Printed in the United States of America

ISBN: 978-1-7373842-4-3 (paperback)
ISBN: 978-1-7373842-5-0 (ebook)

All rights reserved solely by the author. The author guarantees all contents are original and do not infringe upon the legal rights of any other person or work. No part of this book may be reproduced in any form without the permission of the author.

Scripture quotations marked (NIV) are taken from the Holy Bible, New International Version®, NIV®. Copyright © 1973, 1978, 1984, 2011 by Biblica, Inc.™ Used by permission of Zondervan. All rights reserved worldwide. www.zondervan.com The "NIV" and "New International Version" are trademarks registered in the United States Patent and Trademark Office by Biblica, Inc.™

Scripture quotations marked (TLB) are taken from The Living Bible copyright © 1971. Used by permission of Tyndale House Publishers, Carol Stream, Illinois 60188. All rights reserved.

Scripture quotations marked (ESV) are from The Holy Bible, English Standard Version® (ESV®). Copyright © 2001 by Crossway, a publishing ministry of Good News Publishers. Used by permission. All rights reserved.

Scripture quotations marked (NKJV) are from the New King James Version®. Copyright © 1982 by Thomas Nelson, Inc. Used by permission. All rights reserved.

Scripture quotations marked (NLV) are from the New Life Version © Christian Literature International. Used by permission. All rights reserved.

ACKNOWLEDGMENTS

First and foremost, thank you, God, for allowing me to write this book to bring You glory.

Thank you Megan Davis and Luke Fisher for your editing skills. You are awesome.

I have been truly blessed with a loving family. Their faith and encouragement make me believe I can do anything.

As devastating as the death of my husband Jerry Fisher was, it awakened my grieving heart to the healing power of nature, proving once again that, yes, God does hear our cries and provides a way through our pain.

Thank you, God, for creating such wonderful places for me to take pictures.

The cover photo was taken in Howard County, MD.

Most of the photos in this book were taken at my home, and I am so thankful God has placed me somewhere so amazing. Photos taken elsewhere include:

Page 9 Carroll County, MD

Page 11 Howard County, MD

Page 19 Letchworth State Park, NY

Page 27 Gamber, MD

Page 45 Howard County, MD

Page 59 Assateague, MD

Page 79 Howard County, MD

Page 89 Howard County, MD

Page 91 Brookside Gardens, Wheaton, MD

Page 93 Eldersburg, MD

Page 95 Howard County, MD

Page 99 Carroll County, MD

DEDICATION

I dedicate this book to Marge Streicker,
and to all the Marge Streickers of the world.
Thank you for hearing the voice of God
and acting upon it.

INTRODUCTION

With billions of voices calling out to God, how is it conceivable He can hear me? I don't know how, but I know He does.

When I was twenty-eight years old, I was involved in a car accident. The woman who hit me was in a hurry to get her brakes fixed. As she sped down the windy country road, she was unaware that around the curve there were three stopped cars. She plowed into me with such force the backseat slammed into my back. I was in the car alone, and yet I felt a hand on my chest preventing me from flying through the windshield. (This was before seatbelts were required.) For the next five years I was unable to work. Pain became my closest friend.

At the time, I was a single mom. Suddenly I was not only unable to work, but also in unimaginable pain. Belonging to a good church is truly a blessing from God. The women of Reisterstown Bible Church cleaned my house, did our laundry, and fixed our dinner. The men picked up my son for church and took him on outings so he wasn't stranded with me.

The accident happened in October. November was a hard month, but the bills were paid. Then came December. There was no money for bills or food, much less Christmas presents. A month before the accident, I had a Christmas Around the World party and sold so much I was able to get everyone on my Christmas list a present, including a bike for my son, for free. My sister, Sharon, and brother-in-law showed up with a Christmas tree. I was short one hundred dollars for rent. A Christmas card arrived from a friend's father with one hundred dollars inside. God was truly taking care of everything.

Of all the amazing things that happened during that time, there is one miracle that stands out more than anything else. I was out of bread and milk and had no way of getting it. I was trying to figure out what I could give Ben for breakfast or put in his lunch for school when someone knocked on the door. My friend Marge Streicker stood there with bread and milk. She actually apologized for not being able to do more. Until the day I die, I will always see her as the angel who bought me bread and milk. Her simple act of kindness showed me that God really does hear my voice in the billions of voices crying out for Him.

Good morning, God. The sun shines through the window, showing me You have gifted me with another day. Yesterday is gone. I can do nothing to change it, but today, with Your help, I have the power to make it special. Help me remember within those billions of voices calling out to You, my voice is unique to You and You do hear me. I am not alone. Thank You for taking my hand and walking into this day with me. Help me make this day a blessing to You.

A New Day

With the rising of the sun and the opening of your eyes, God is handing you a gift, the gift of a new day. You and only you decide what to do with that gift. Will you embrace it with joy and thankfulness or shuffle through letting everything aggravate you? It is your choice. God lovingly handed you this day. Your gift to Him is what you make it. Make it great.

A New Day

*"It is of the Lord's mercies that we are not consumed, because his compassions fail not.
They are new every morning; great is thy faithfulness."*
Lamentations 3:22-23 (KJV)

With the morning light, a freshness fills the air. The sky is full of rays of love and forgiveness. Yesterday's mistakes are gone. Today is a new day. Take a deep breath. Fill your heart with God's love. Allow it to wash away your sins. Forgive yourself as God forgave you. Today is a new day. Embrace it with love.

A New Day

"I have swept away your offenses like a cloud, your sins like the morning mist.
Return to me, for I have redeemed you."
Isaiah 44:22 (NIV)

Greet each day like a bird singing hallelujah. It knows not what the day will bring, but it does know that by filling the earth with a joyful noise, the day will be great. Embrace the morning light with thankfulness. Take a deep breath; fill your soul with happiness. A day embraced with love will have the strength to handle any hurdles that follow.

A New Day

"Sing to the Lord a new song; sing to the Lord, all the earth."
Psalm 96:1 (NIV)

Hello, God. Can You hear me? I come to You asking for guidance for those who are unsure of their purpose. So many people believe they have no reason for being here, other than taking up space. Help them realize it is not the amount of ability one has that defines one's purpose. For we all are given the same goal: to bring glory to Your name. Help them understand that a simple act of kindness is as meaningful as someone whose purpose seems bigger than life. Thank you, God, for using us to show the world Your love.

Purpose

There is no such thing as "the impossible dream." Dreams are the voice of your subconscious showing you what the future could hold. If God gave you the desire, He gave you the means to achieve it. You are only limited by your faith in yourself. Every one of us has a purpose, a dream instilled in us before we were born. Keep striving for your dream and before you know it, you will blossom for all the world to see.

Purpose

"The Lord of hosts hath sworn, saying, Surely as I have thought,
so shall it come to pass; and as I have purposed, so shall it stand."
Isaiah 14:24 (KJV)

The cold harsh winter did everything it could to stop the river from flowing. And yet, a part of it refuses to give in to the arctic temperature. The waterfall, though mostly frozen, has not given up its purpose. It still flows in the middle of the frozen water.

When life does its best to stop you, keep moving forward, even if it looks impossible. Draw strength from the waterfalls and continue to flow toward your goal.

Purpose

"You need to persevere so that when you have done the will of God, you will receive what He has promised."
Hebrews 10:36 (NIV)

Every seed has a reason for being. However, until it is planted, its purpose lays dormant. Once planted, it needs to be cultivated. Without water, the seed will die. Without weeding, the seed will be lost in a jungle of unwanted plants, hidden from the world.

God planted the seed of purpose within you. All you need to do is nurture it. He equipped you with all you need to fulfill your destiny. What is stopping you?

Purpose

"I cry out to God Most High, to God who fulfills his purpose for me."
Psalm 57:2 (ESV)

Hello, God. Can You hear me? Every moment of every day there are choices to be made, choices I don't even realize I'm making. Like the choice to get out of bed, to go to work, to eat, to smile, to laugh… simple little choices I make every day without thought.

Dear Heavenly Father, help me remember that when I waste time on the internet, that is a choice I made. When I get angry, that is a choice I made. When I take time to admire Your handywork, that is a choice I made. Please guide me through this day. Allow Your peace to surround me when I make the right choices.

CHOICES

The first thing most people do when they see a bee is get out of its way. The second is to find something to kill it with; no one wants to be stung. As annoying as bees are, they are an important part of life. They work hard to bring our food and flowers to life. Like the bee, there are many things in our life that we wish to be rid of... things or people that are bothersome. We see them and we just want to run and hide. Stop for a moment and think. Is there a purpose for this? Instead of cringing the next time you are faced with something or someone irritating, take a moment to ask yourself, "Is it helping me to grow, to learn?" When you choose to look beyond the annoyance, the annoyance becomes a blessing.

Choices

*"We who are strong ought to bear with the failings of the weak and not to please ourselves.
Each of us should please our neighbors for their good, to build them up.
For even Christ did not please himself, but, as it is written:
'The insults of those who insult you have fallen on me.'
For everything that was written in the past was written to teach us,
so that through the endurance taught in the Scriptures and the encouragement they provide
we might have hope. May the God who gives endurance and encouragement
give you the same attitude of mind toward each other that Christ Jesus had,
so that with one mind and one voice you may glorify the God and Father of our Lord Jesus Christ.
Accept one another, then, just as Christ accepted you, in order to bring praise to God."
Romans 15:1-7 (NIV)*

It is so easy to run with the crowd, to get caught up in the emotions of the moment even if you know deep inside of you it's wrong. Standing up for your principles is hard. You are ridiculed and made to doubt your beliefs, told you are old-fashioned, times have changed. The truth never changes. It is there for all times. Being true to yourself will become a beacon of hope to others.

"Whoever walks with the wise becomes wise, but the companion of fools will suffer harm. Disaster pursues sinners, but the righteous are rewarded with good."
Proverbs 13:20-21 (ESV)

The butterfly is drawn by the beauty of the milkweed, choosing to land on it instead of the daisy. You, like the butterfly, are making choices every day without even realizing you are doing so. From the moment you opened your eyes, you started to make choices. However, the most important choice of your day is one you didn't make. It was made by God—the choice to give you another day. How are you going to choose to live this day?

Choices

"This is the day that the Lord has made; let us rejoice and be glad in it."
Psalm 118:24 (ESV)

Hello, God. Can You hear me? I'm so tired of running into obstacles. I just want to throw my hands up in defeat. Every time things are going smoothly, another problem appears to stop me. Please give me the wisdom and strength to continue on.

OBSTACLES

Unlike the sunflowers nearby, this sunflower is twisted and close to the earth. Nature did its best to knock it to the ground. It did not grow tall and strong, and yet it still produced a flower. Of all the sunflowers, this one is the most amazing. It has to fight the shadows of the sunflowers beside it to see the sun... but it does.

Is a handicap holding you back? Whether it's physical, emotional, financial, educational, or health issues, you can overcome the challenge. Someone somewhere in the world, with the same handicap as you, has already proven it can be done. When life tries to beat you down, bloom anyway. What a wonderful feeling it is to complete a task when it looks like everything is against you. Obstacles make us stronger. When the journey is done, the beauty of the job speaks for itself. I believe in you. But most importantly, God believes in you.

Obstacles

"...but we rejoice in our sufferings, knowing that suffering produces endurance,
and endurance produces character, and character produces hope,
and hope does not put us to shame, because God's love has been poured into our hearts
through the Holy Spirit who has been given to us."
Romans 5:3-5 (ESV)

Fear is one of the biggest obstacles we face. The raccoon clings to the tree in fright, allowing the distress of being seen to paralyze him in place, when in reality, all he has to do is climb up and over into another tree to make his escape. There was no real danger, only imaginary.

Most of the fears in life never happen. They are worries we make up in our head, and yet we cling to them like the raccoon clinging to the tree.

What are you afraid of? Are you letting it paralyze you in place? Release the grip of fear into God's hand. Feel the burden of anxieties fall away one step at a time.

Obstacles

"Fear thou not; for I am with thee: be not dismayed; for I am thy God: I will strengthen thee; yea, I will help thee; yea, I will uphold thee with the right hand of my righteousness."
Isaiah 41:10 (KJV)

The tree once stood strong and tall, giving shade and shelter to the animals in the woods. Then a storm came along and dropped it to the ground. The tree did not deserve to fall, nor did it fall due to something it did. But as it laid on the ground, an amazing thing happened. It found a new purpose, a new way to spread beauty.

Like the tree, life can knock you to the ground, leaving you calling out to God in anguish, "Why God, why? What did I do to deserve this?" The true question should be, "How can I turn this to the glory of God?" There is no obstacle God cannot overcome. Call out to God. Let Him reach down and lift you from the ground.

Obstacles

*"These things I have spoken unto you, that in me ye might have peace.
In the world ye shall have tribulation: but be of good cheer;
I have overcome the world."*
John 16:33 (KJV)

Hello, God. Can You hear me? I am trying so hard to not hang on to the past, but it seems impossible. How can I forget what happened? How can I believe the future won't be more of the same? Please help me release the past into Your hands, to know the peace of a future with Your hope.

The Past

Are you daydreaming about the past? *What if I had... My life would be so different if I had...* The past is the past, and whatever path you took was the right one. It might not be easy and maybe it will take twice as long to get where you want to be, but never forget that it was you who made the choice. You might have been influenced by others, but it was you who made the final decision. If it was supposed to be, it would be. Stop dreaming about the "what ifs." They are gone. Start dreaming of the future and what it holds for you. The possibilities are endless as long as your focus is forward.

The Past

*"Remember ye not the former things, neither consider the things of old.
Behold, I will do a new thing; now it shall spring forth; shall ye not know it?
I will even make a way in the wilderness, and rivers in the desert."*
Isaiah 43:18-19 (KJV)

The daffodil is trying hard to escort spring into full bloom, but winter is doing its best to stop it. The winter, like the past, is not ready to let go. Until it is gone, new life cannot emerge.

Treat the past like melting snow; it was nice while it lasted, but its time is done. Don't let the past hold you back. It had its season. Now it is time to let go and allow new life to spring forth.

The Past

*"Behold, the former things have come to pass, and new things I now declare;
Before they spring forth I tell you of them."*
Isaiah 42:9 (ESV)

Is yesterday holding you back from embracing the joys of life? Hanging on to the past is like a tree clinging on to last year's leaves. As long as it holds on to the dead leaves, new growth cannot begin. When other trees are embracing the rebirth of spring, it stubbornly holds on to the past. The past is behind you; let it go. Drop those dead leaves, no matter how painful. Only by doing so will you be able to embrace the joys of the life awaiting you.

The Past

*"Brethren, I count myself to have apprehended: but this one thing I do,
forgetting those things which are behind,
and reaching forth unto those things which are before."*
Philippians 3:13 (KJV)

Hello, God. Can You hear me? I try very hard to be positive, but sometimes I feel such anger inside of me. The negativity of the world engulfs me like a dark pit. I just want to scream, but that isn't the person I want to be. Please help me embrace all that is good in the world, and acknowledge the bad without holding on to it. Help me put the negative thoughts behind me, and push the positive into the light of day.

NEGATIVITY

Negative words are lies of Satan made for one purpose only—to damage the truth. Words like *stupid*, *worthless*, and *ugly* are words that might have the power to destroy you one bruise at a time. For years, I struggled with the negative lies I had been told, allowing those words to reign in my life. Until the day I realized with each lie believed, I was destroying who God created me to be. The truth is you are a beautiful creation of God. He designed you to bring glory to the world. Your worth is beyond priceless.

Negativity

"For you formed my inward parts; you knitted me together in my mother's womb. I praise you, for I am fearfully and wonderfully made. Wonderful are your works; my soul knows it very well. My frame was not hidden from you, when I was being made in secret, intricately woven in the depths of the earth."
Psalm 139:13-15 (ESV)

What seemed like a disaster ended up being a blessing. The fire burned through the field, leaving only a charred mess. Within a week, nature started showing signs of a rebirth, and before long, the field was covered in milkweed, a haven for butterflies.

Out of ashes came beauty. The pain of life's disasters can leave us feeling as if all is lost. Take courage from the fields. You too can rejuvenate and heal. Hold your head up. Emerge from the fire with dignity and beauty.

Negativity

"In all this you greatly rejoice, though now for a little while you may have had to suffer grief in all kinds of trials. These have come so that the proven genuineness of your faith— of greater worth than gold, which perishes even though refined by fire— may result in praise, glory and honor when Jesus Christ is revealed."
1 Peter 1:6-7 (NIV)

The woodpecker gets a bad rap for destroying trees. The reality is that the woodpecker is the secondary problem; he would not be tapping holes in the tree if there were not bugs inside of it. The bugs are weakening the tree from the inside out. The woodpecker is actually trying to solve the issue, but in the process, it is compounding it.

Often the real pains of life are hidden beneath the surface, causing us to put the responsibility in the wrong place.

Are you putting the blame in the wrong place? Have you looked beyond the surface for the real root of trouble? Only when you discover the true problem can it be solved.

Negativity

"Let no one say when he is tempted, 'I am being tempted by God,'
for God cannot be tempted with evil, and he himself tempts no one.
But each person is tempted when he is lured and enticed by his own desire.
Then desire when it has conceived gives birth to sin,
and sin when it is fully grown brings forth death."
James 1:13-15 (ESV)

Whenever I see pictures of Adam and Even naked in the garden, my first thought is that they obviously were not allergic to poison ivy. Those who catch poison ivy know how evil it is. Life has taught me where there is evil, there is also good. With poison, that good comes in the form of jewelweed, a wonderful plant that grows right beside the poison ivy. Jewelweed not only stops the pain, but also prevents you from getting it. The most amazing thing to me is how God can use a simple weed to bring relief to an itchy, achy, miserable body. Can you imagine how much more He can do to a spirit looking for relief? No matter what evil may have formed against you, know this: God has a plan in place to see you through it.

In this world, just like the jewelweed and the poison ivy, good and evil live side by side. Like unseen poison, sin can creep up on us and mar our souls with festering sores. The soul that aches feels defeated and ashamed. Beside each sin there is a way to redemption—God's love. Call out to Him. Ask Him to open not only your eyes, but also your heart to the grace of forgiveness. Allow your aching soul to be touched by the miracle of God.

*"No weapon that is formed against thee shall prosper;
and every tongue that shall rise against thee in judgment thou shalt condemn.
This is the heritage of the servants of the Lord,
and their righteousness is of me, saith the Lord."*
Isaiah 54:17 (KJV)

Hello, God. Can You hear me? Your word says, *"If you have faith as small as a mustard seed, you can say to this mountain, 'Move from here to there,' and it will move. Nothing will be impossible for you."* I truly believe that with all my heart, and yet, time and time again, I fall flat on my face. Tears of frustration from another failure consume me and I lash out at You. Please forgive my temper tantrum. Help me remember You are in control of all things. My faith is good enough and this too will somehow work out.

FRUSTRATION

The Assateague pony is frustrated with the woman taking his picture and is ready to charge the offender. He just wants to eat the grass and be left alone. You can almost hear him snorting, "Leave me alone."

How often do we let little transgressions get under our skin? Frustration is a weapon Satan uses to slowly destroy our peace. He just slowly picks away until we are yelling to be left alone. When you feel the bubbles of frustration forming, say a quick prayer, take a deep breath, and know that God will handle this too, no matter how small the offenses.

Frustration

"Cast all your anxiety on him because he cares for you. Be alert and of sober mind. Your enemy the devil prowls around like a roaring lion looking for someone to devour. Resist him, standing firm in the faith, because you know that the family of believers throughout the world is undergoing the same kind of sufferings."
1 Peter 5:7-9 (NIV)

Geese fly south for the winter. This pair made a late start and now they are faced with the harsh reality of winter. Instead of allowing the frustration of the situation to dampen their spirits, they chose to enjoy the snow.

Negativity sneaks up on us like a cold winter storm, leaving us emotionally snowbound. Instead of allowing negative thoughts to cripple you, put a spin on them. Find something in there that you can shine new light on. Remember there is nothing on earth that can defeat you, not even negativity. You have the power through Jesus to conquer all.

Frustration

"My brethren, count it all joy when ye fall into diverse temptations;
Knowing this, that the trying of your faith worketh patience.
But let patience have her perfect work, that ye may be perfect and entire, wanting nothing."
James 1:2-4 (KJV)

Weeds and dead leaves threaten to overtake the sunflower. But it refuses to allow the frustrations of nature to defeat its true purpose—to bring beauty where there was none. Frustrations can appear out of nowhere, causing anxiety to rule over reason. Once allowed to swirl through your mind, it is very easy to become defeated. Do not allow it to stop you in your tracks. Deep inside of you, you know you can fight through the mist of frustrations. Hold your head up and grab hold of the beauty in the chaos.

Frustration

*"The Lord your God in your midst, the Mighty One, will save;
He will rejoice over you with gladness, He will quiet you with His love,
He will rejoice over you with singing."*
Zephaniah 3:17 (NKJV)

Jake the goat is a master of escape, but on this day his jump to freedom was cut short. He cried for help and patiently waited for it to arrive. He did not fight the fence, or the helping hands that freed him. His plan did not go as easily as he had hoped, but in the end he still got where he wanted to be, eating apples from the tree.

Frustration comes when you know your idea is going to work. It can't fail, and yet, it does. Once again, you find yourself hanging on for dear life and the only thing you can do is yell for help.

Through the tears and pain of yet another failed attempt, you might find yourself lashing out at those around you, including God. When the crying has stopped, take a lesson from the goat. Not all things go as planned, but God does hear your cry and will help you get where you need to be.

*"When I said, 'My foot is slipping,' your love, O Lord, supported me
When anxiety was great within me, your consolation brought joy to my soul."*
Psalm 94:18-19 (NIV)

Frustration

Hello, God. Can You hear me? I'm falling on my knees begging for answers. Why, God? Why? I don't understand why accidents happen. Why do diseases destroy our lives? Why do loved ones leave? I have never felt such overwhelming pain. Every part of me hurts. This pain is more than I can bear. How am I supposed to go on? Please, I beg of You, help me through this agony.

GRIEF

The agony of grief is overwhelming. It consumes us like a vacuum of darkness, an emotion not unknown to God. Before Jesus died, there was total darkness for three hours, and the moment He died on the cross there was an earthquake. God's grief manifested for the world to see. His son died because of the evil in the world. Jesus didn't deserve to die, but He did. Three days later, He arose, conquering death for us all.

The pain of grief never leaves us. It is a wound upon the heart that we learn to live with. The scar of grief is there because you loved. It is that love that will see you through your darkest hours. The scars of life are a beautiful gift; embrace the memories. Breathe, be strong, call on the comfort of God, and allow Him to wrap His loving arms around you. The darkness will fade and the light will shine again.

Grief

*"Why art thou cast down, O my soul? And why art thou disquieted in me?
Hope thou in God: for I shall yet praise him for the help of his countenance."*
Psalm 42:5 (KJV)

Like storm clouds rolling in, the loss of a loved one, whether through death or simply someone walking away, leaves us feeling like there is a hole in our heart. It is so easy to allow the dark clouds to take control, but once that happens, fighting your way out of the darkness begins to feel like an impossible journey.

The holes left in your heart are not empty. They are filled with loving memories. It's a wonderful legacy to leave someone a heart planted with love. How awesome is it that throughout their lives, those we loved were leaving deposits of love to be cashed in when the holes began to appear? Each hole is no longer dark. Instead, inside is a beautiful flower planted by loved ones to fill those holes.

As you go through life, the best you can hope to do is plant tiny seeds of love along the way. When you are gone, those seeds will blossom into a beautiful bouquet in the heart of your loved ones, dimming the ache they feel. Love is the greatest gift you can leave someone.

Grief

"The Lord is near to the brokenhearted, and saves the crushed in spirit."
Psalm 34:18 (RSV)

I can think of no emotion as devastating as grief. Not only does it break your heart, but it also pierces your soul to the point of bringing you to your knees, broken and twisted up inside. Each breath and each step takes such an effort that you long to just quit living.

Within the darkness of grief, there is life. Your life. As hard as it is, you can survive the darkness. Honor the loss of a loved one by living.

Grief

"And God shall wipe away all tears from their eyes; and there shall be no more death, neither sorrow, nor crying, neither shall there be any more pain: for the former things are passed away."
Revelation 21:4 (KJV)

When Lazarus died, Jesus cried. Why would He cry, knowing He was about to raise Lazarus from the dead? Jesus cried because the grief of His friends was so heartbreaking.

When you experience the anguish of grief, Jesus feels it, too. Your tears mingle with His. Jesus mourned, then moved on with life. You too need to cry, to allow the tears to wash the pain of sorrow from your heart. The sun will shine again, the tears will stop, and the love will forever live on in the beauty of your soul.

Grief

"Jesus said unto her, 'I am the resurrection, and the life:
he that believeth in me, though he were dead, yet shall he live'."
John 11:25 (KJV)

Hello, God. Can You hear me? Waves of darkness threaten to overcome me. I feel scared, alone, and unworthy. Getting out of bed is a struggle. I pray for the darkness of my depression to be touched by Your hand. I know You are mightier than any enemy, and with Your loving help I can overcome this. Touch my mind and make me whole.

DEPRESSION

Everything is great. Your life seems to be on the right track and then, like a lurking monster, depression hits you. Suicidal thoughts replace laughter. Loneliness replaces friends. All you want to do is crawl up into a little ball and die. You struggle to find a reason to live. Your every thought is that those around you would be better off without you. That is just where Satan wants you to be. He wants you to feel defeated. He wants to stop you from achieving greatness.

What better way to throw someone off track than to turn off the lights. You must be destined for something great; otherwise, the devil would have no time for you. Think about it. If you really were worthless, if no one cared about you, if there was no reason to live, why would Satan torment you? You would be no danger to him. He would just let you go on your uneventful way. But none of that is true. You are worthwhile. You are loved. You have a purpose in life. And what a great one it must be to have Satan trying to torment you into defeat. Stand up to him and call out to Jesus. Fight the darkness with light. Satan cannot put out the light of God no matter how hard he tries.

You are strong. You are worthy of happiness. You are destined for greatness.

Depression

"The thief cometh not, but for to steal, and to kill, and to destroy."
John 10:10 (KJV)

The praying mantis does not focus on the few dead blossoms, nor does it think of how soon all the flowers will be dead. No. If it did, depression would quickly follow. Instead, it embraces the beauty there now. It basks in the joy around it.

Throughout each day, bad things happen. You can focus on them, or you can be like the praying mantis and embrace the good things. Happiness isn't dependent on the perfect job, marriage, relationship, house, or children. Most people's picture-perfect world is as shallow as the canvas it's painted on. How is your canvas? Is it the way you pictured it? If not, repaint it. You have the power within you to achieve happiness. Happiness is real and it's there for you. Reach down inside of you and make it happen. Do not say, "Tomorrow I will be happy." Say, "Today I am happy." Embrace the beauty of each day and allow it to fill you with joy.

Depression

"I know that there is nothing better for people than to be happy and to do good while they live. That each of them may eat and drink, and find satisfaction in all their toil—this is the gift of God."
Ecclesiastes 3:12-13 (NIV)

Depression is like storm clouds threatening to devour everything in their path. Out of nowhere, depression converges upon you, sending you huddling into darkness.

It is a struggle so many people have had, including Elijah and King David. Both men were overcome with depression, and relied on God to see them through it.

When the darkness of depression rolls in, call out to God. Allow Him to lift you up from the pit of darkness. He will save you.

Depression

*"I waited patiently for the Lord; he turned to me and heard my cry.
He lifted me out of the slimy pit, out of the mud and mire; he set my feet on a rock
and gave me a firm place to stand. He put a new song in my mouth,
a hymn of praise to our God. Many will see and fear the Lord and put their trust in him."*
Psalm 40:1-3 (NIV)

Hello, God. Can You hear me? The day has just begun and I already feel worn out. I don't know how I'm going to get everything I'm supposed to do, done. Day after day it's the same thing. I just keep going until I collapse into bed. Please help me stop saying yes to everything. Help me not feel guilty for taking a moment to rest. Renew my spirit.

Rest

In our fast-paced world, it is hard to take time to slow down and relax. As we run around trying to attain the perfect life, we often get overwhelmed. Love and thankfulness are replaced with stress. We keep going until we fall into bed exhausted. There is no time to rest. But you must.

Take a few moments tonight and look at the night sky. Right before it rests for the night, the sky does one final light show. Allow the beautifully lit sky to relax your spirit and reenergize you for the work ahead.

Rest

"Be careful for nothing; but in every thing by prayer and supplication with thanksgiving let your requests be known unto God. And the peace of God, which passeth all understanding shall keep your hearts and minds through Christ Jesus."
Philippians 4:6-7 (KJV)

Have you ever watched a butterfly? Even when it is on a flower, its wings move. The butterfly works hard at its pollinating job. It flutters from flower to flower until the end of the day when it finally finds a place to rest.

Are you like the butterfly, flitting from task to task, never taking a moment to rest? When you keep going and going, you tumble into bed at the end of the day too exhausted to sleep.

Life is busy, but finding even fifteen minutes to enjoy the beauty around you can rejuvenate your soul and make it leap with joy. God placed a beautiful world around you. Enjoy it.

Rest

"It is senseless for you to work so hard from early morning until late at night, fearing you will starve to death; for God wants his loved ones to get their proper rest."
Psalm 127:2 (TLB)

Hello, God. Can You hear me? I want to feel Your love like I did as a child. When love is around, the day seems brighter, the world seems happier, and life is better. Those little things that bother me don't seem to bother me anymore. Please fill my heart with love for others, love for myself, and love for You.

LOVE

As a child, I didn't try to figure out why Jesus loved me. He just did. The simple faith of a child is the true example of unconditional faith. Somewhere along the road, that simple faith became complicated. My heart says Jesus loves me, but my brain asks how that is possible. He sees my sins. He knows my thoughts. He sees every time I slip back into the tidal wave of defeat. How can Jesus love me?

The truth of Jesus's love is that He knew before He got on the cross that I was a sinner, and yet He bore my sins away. He tells me over and over that His love is unconditional. His love will never change. It's my perception that clouds the way. The perception of looking at love through my eyes and not the eyes of the Lord. Thus, with the simple faith of a child and the knowledge of an adult, I will embrace the love that is freely given to all who accept it, the undying love of Jesus. With that love comes freedom. The freedom to have unconditional faith. I pray that you too will embrace the love of Jesus with the heart of a child.

Love

"But God shows his love for us in that while we were still sinners, Christ died for us."
Romans 5:8 (NIV)

Do you ever wonder if God really loves you? Look around and you will clearly see the answer. Twice a day His artwork fills the sky. Morning and night, a symphony of song fills the air. Flowers grace our day with color and a sweet fragrance that no perfume can equal. Animals run with the joy of being alive.

God didn't have to make the world a beautiful place. He didn't have to send His son, Jesus, to die on the cross for us, but He did. Why? Because He loves us. Awaken your mind to the true beauty of nature, the voice of God saying, "I love you."

Love

*"For God so loved the world, that he gave his only begotten Son,
that whosoever believeth in him should not perish, but have everlasting life."*
John 3:16 (KJV)

The beauty of nature is its diversity and how it all blends together in peace and harmony. Like nature, God created you, your neighbor, and the stranger you pass on the street. Your differences are not meant to separate you, but to make life stronger. Each person is unique in his or her own way. When we work together, love flourishes. The beauty of life is that no matter how different you may be, Jesus loves you. When we allow His love into our hearts, all things are possible.

Love

"Above all, love each other deeply, because love covers over a multitude of sins."
1 Peter 4:8 (NIV)

As the sun sets on the day, fill your heart with mercy. Release the pain of the day into the light, allowing the last ray of sunshine to evaporate any wrongs. Everyone at some point in time will do something to upset someone else, whether intentional or not. You can choose to hold on to the offense or forgive it. I like to imagine that I'm putting my hurt feelings in a box and laying it at God's feet. If I bring it into the next day, then I really haven't give it to God. Forgiveness is the greatest form of love. Fill your heart with love and let God do the rest.

Love

"Therefore, I tell you, her many sins have been forgiven—as her great love has shown. But whoever has been forgiven little loves little. Then Jesus said to her, 'Your sins are forgiven'."
Luke 7:47-48 (NIV)

Thank you for reading *Hello God, Can You Hear Me?* I may not know your name, but rest assured I will be praying for you tonight as I do for all my readers. I pray you find the strength to handle whatever problems you are facing and that you too will see the love of God pouring out from above in the beauty of His nature, proving how much He cares for you.

Books by Vickie Fisher

Hello God, Are You There?
Hello God, It's Me Again
Hello God, Can You Hear Me?

Contact the author at Vickie.fisher@verizon.net
Web page: Vickiefisher.com